AIR FRYER RECIPES
FOR BEGINNERS

*Recipes for Appetizing Dishes for
a Healthy Lifestyle*

SAM HAMIL

Table of Contents

Sommario

Introduction

What is an air fryer?

It is an appliance that typically has an egg shape, more or less square, with a removable basket in which you put the food to be cooked. It takes advantage of the concept of air cooking at high temperatures that reach up to 200° allowing a healthy "frying-not-frying" of fresh food. Abandon, then, the thought of frying in which the food is immersed in a lot of oil because the amount of oil used inside the air fryer can be as little as a couple of teaspoons of spray. True frying in lots of hot oil is practically "dangerous", especially in case you abuse it or don't pay proper attention. In the air fryer, the oil will never reach the smoke point and is therefore not harmful.

The hot air, which reaches high temperatures, circulates in the compartment of the air fryer allowing even cooking of food both outside and inside. This way you can cook meat, fish, vegetables and thousands of other dishes in no time - in short, you can prepare many recipes with the air fryer. Meat cooked in the air fryer is succulent, tender, and soft, excess fat runs off and does not remain inside the meat giving it an exceptional flavor.

The air fryer also works as an oven and grill...

The air fryer is very different and in addition to its main purpose, the air cooking of food for a light and healthy fried, it is also an appliance that serves as an oven for gratin for different recipes, pasta dishes, vegetables, to prepare cakes and pies of all kinds, muffins, buns, pizzas. It has been shown that in the best performing models, the air fryer allows eliminating excess fat, even up to 50%, without altering the flavor of food, giving the right friability typical of fried foods.

Which air fryer to choose to buy?

For air fryer selection, the suggestion could also be a reliable product to urge better and better results. A high-quality product makes an equivalent quality product. Therefore, it would be fair to consider spending a bit more on a much better-performing air fryer that also has better quality materials. However, depending on your needs, many excellent products are affordable.

Now you just need to take a look at the air fryer recipes. They are all proven, safe and outstanding recipes!

Chicken

Thanksgiving Turkey with Mint Sauce

(Ready in about 1 hour | Servings 3)

368 Calories; 11.8g Fat; 11.3g Carbs; 54g Protein; 1.8g Sugars

Ingredients

1 ½ pounds turkey tenderloin
1 teaspoon olive oil
Sea salt and black pepper, to season
1 teaspoon dried thyme
1/2 teaspoon garlic powder
1/2 teaspoon dried sage
Sauce:
2 slices white bread
3/4 ounce fresh mint leaves
1 tablespoon extra-virgin olive oil
1 tablespoon white wine vinegar
1 teaspoon garlic, minced

Directions

Toss the turkey tenderloin with olive oil, salt, pepper, thyme, garlic powder and sage.
Cook in the preheated Air Fryer at 350 degrees F for about 55 minutes, turning it over halfway through the cooking time.
Meanwhile, make the mint sauce; pulse the bread slices in a food processor until coarsely crumbled.
Add in the mint, olive oil, vinegar and garlic; blend again until everything is well incorporated; make sure to add water slowly and gradually until your desired consistency is reached.
Let it rest on a wire rack to cool slightly before carving and serving.
Spoon the sauce over warm turkey and serve. Bon appétit!

Adobo Seasoned Chicken with Veggies

(Ready in about 1 hour 30 minutes | Servings 4)

427 Calories; 15.3g Fat; 18.5g Carbs; 52.3g Protein; 9.4g Sugars

Ingredients

2 pounds chicken wings, rinsed and patted dry
1 teaspoon coarse sea salt
1/4 teaspoon ground black pepper
1/2 teaspoon red pepper flakes, crushed
1 teaspoon ground cumin
1 teaspoon paprika
1 teaspoon granulated onion
1 teaspoon ground turmeric
2 tablespoons tomato powder
1 tablespoon dry Madeira wine
2 stalks celery, diced
2 cloves garlic, peeled but not chopped
1 large Spanish onion, diced
2 bell peppers, seeded and sliced
4 carrots, trimmed and halved
2 tablespoons olive oil

Directions

Toss all ingredients in a large bowl. Cover and let it sit for 1 hour in your refrigerator.
Add the chicken wings to a baking pan.
Roast the chicken wings in the preheated Air Fryer at 380 degrees F for 7 minutes.
Add the vegetables and cook an additional 15 minutes, shaking the basket once or twice. Serve warm.

Paprika Chicken Legs with Brussels Sprouts

(Ready in about 30 minutes | Servings 2)

355 Calories; 20.1g Fat; 5.3g Carbs; 36.6g Protein; 0.2g Sugars

Ingredients

2 chicken legs
1/2 teaspoon paprika
1/2 teaspoon kosher salt
1/2 teaspoon black pepper
1 pound Brussels sprouts
1 teaspoon dill, fresh or dried

Directions

Start by preheating your Air Fryer to 370 degrees F.
Now, season your chicken with paprika, salt, and pepper. Transfer the chicken legs to the cooking basket. Cook for 10 minutes.
Flip the chicken legs and cook an additional 10 minutes. Reserve.
Add the Brussels sprouts to the cooking basket; sprinkle with dill.
Cook at 380 degrees F for 15 minutes, shaking the basket halfway through.
Serve with the reserved chicken legs. Bon appétit!

Roast Turkey

(Ready in about 50 minutes | Servings 6)

316 Calories; 24.2g Fat; 2.5g Carbs; 20.4g Protein; 1.1g Sugars

Ingredients

1 pounds turkey
1 tablespoon fresh rosemary, chopped
1 teaspoon sea salt
1/2 teaspoon ground black pepper
1 onion, chopped
1 celery stalk, chopped

Directions

Start by preheating your Air Fryer to 360 degrees F. Spritz the sides and bottom of the cooking basket with a nonstick cooking spray. Place the turkey in the cooking basket. Add the rosemary, salt, and black pepper. Cook for 30 minutes in the preheated Air Fryer. Add the onion and celery and cook an additional 15 minutes. Bon appétit!

Italian Chicken and Cheese Frittata

(Ready in about 25 minutes | Servings 4)

329 Calories; 25.3g Fat; 3.4g Carbs; 21.1g Protein; 2.3g Sugars

Ingredients

1 (1-pound) fillet chicken breast
Sea salt and ground black pepper, to taste
1 tablespoon olive oil
4 eggs
1/2 teaspoon cayenne pepper
1/2 cup Mascarpone cream
1/4 cup Asiago cheese, freshly grated

Directions

Flatten the chicken breast with a meat mallet. Season with salt and
pepper.
Heat the olive oil in a frying pan over medium flame. Cook the
chicken for 10 to 12 minutes; slice into small strips, and reserve.
Then, in a mixing bowl, thoroughly combine the eggs, and cayenne
pepper; season with salt to taste. Add the cheese and stir to combine.
Add the reserved chicken. Then, pour the mixture into a lightly
greased pan; put the pan into the cooking basket.
Cook in the preheated Air Fryer at 355 degrees F for 10 minutes,
flipping over halfway through.

Pork

Herb-Crusted Pork Roast

(Ready in about 1 hour | Servings 2)

220 Calories; 11.4g Fat; 3.3g Carbs; 24.9g Protein; 1.7g Sugars

Ingredients

1/2 pound pork loin
Salt and black pepper, to taste
1/2 teaspoon onion powder
1/2 teaspoon parsley flakes
1/2 teaspoon oregano
1/2 teaspoon thyme
1/2 teaspoon grated lemon peel
1 teaspoon garlic, minced
1 teaspoon butter, softened

Directions

Pat the pork loin dry with kitchen towels. Season it with salt and black pepper.
In a bowl, mix the remaining ingredients until well combined.
Coat the pork with the herb rub, pressing to adhere well.
Cook in the preheated Air Fryer at 360 degrees F for 30 minutes; turn it over and cook on the other side for 25 minutes more. Bon appétit!

Omelet with Prosciutto and Ricotta Cheese

(Ready in about 15 minutes | Servings 2)

389 Calories; 28.8g Fat; 3.2g Carbs; 29.1g Protein; 0.5g Sugars

Ingredients

2 tablespoons olive oil
4 eggs
2 tablespoons scallions, chopped
4 tablespoons Ricotta cheese
1/4 teaspoon black pepper, freshly cracked
Salt, to taste
6 ounces prosciutto, chopped
1 tablespoon Italian parsley, roughly chopped

Directions

Generously grease a baking pan with olive oil.
Then, whisk the eggs, and add the scallions, cheese, black pepper, and salt. Fold in the chopped prosciutto and mix to combine well. Spoon into the prepared baking pan.
Cook in the preheated Air Fryer at 360 F for 6 minutes. Serve immediately garnished with Italian parsley.

Warm Pork Salad

(Ready in about 20 minutes | Servings 3)

315 Calories; 13.3g Fat; 15.5g Carbs; 30.5g Protein; 10.2g Sugars

Ingredients

1 pound pork shoulder, cut into strips
1/4 teaspoon fresh ginger, minced
1 teaspoon garlic, pressed
1 tablespoon olive oil
1 tablespoon honey
2 teaspoons fresh cilantro, chopped
1 tablespoon Worcestershire sauce
1 medium-sized cucumber, sliced
1 cup arugula
1 cup baby spinach
1 cup Romaine lettuce
1 tomato, diced
1 shallot, sliced

Directions

Spritz the Air Fryer cooking basket with a nonstick spray. Place the pork in the Air Fryer cooking basket.
Cook at 400 degrees F for 13 minutes, shaking the basket halfway through the cooking time.
Transfer the meat to a serving bowl and toss with the remaining ingredients.
Bon appétit!

Mexican-Style Ground Pork with Peppers

(Ready in about 40 minutes | Servings 4)

505 Calories; 39.4g Fat; 9.9g Carbs; 28g Protein; 5.1g Sugars

Ingredients

2 chili peppers
1 red bell pepper
2 tablespoons olive oil
1 large-sized shallot, chopped
1 pound ground pork
2 garlic cloves, minced
2 ripe tomatoes, pureed
1 teaspoon dried marjoram
1/2 teaspoon mustard seeds
1/2 teaspoon celery seeds
1 teaspoon Mexican oregano
1 tablespoon fish sauce
2 tablespoons fresh coriander, chopped
Salt and ground black pepper, to taste
2 cups water
1 tablespoon chicken bouillon granules
2 tablespoons sherry wine
1 cup Mexican cheese blend

Directions

Roast the peppers in the preheated Air Fryer at 395 degrees F for 10 minutes, flipping them halfway through cook time.

Let them steam for 10 minutes; then, peel the skin and discard the stems and seeds. Slice the peppers into halves.

Heat the olive oil in a baking pan at 380 degrees F for 2 minutes; add the shallots and cook for 4 minutes. Add the ground pork and garlic; cook for a further 4 to 5 minutes.

After that, stir in the tomatoes, marjoram, mustard seeds, celery seeds, oregano, fish sauce, coriander, salt, and pepper. Add a layer of sliced peppers to the baking pan.

Mix the water with the chicken bouillon granules and sherry wine. Add the mixture to the baking pan.

Cook in the preheated Air Fryer at 395 degrees F for 10 minutes. Top with cheese and bake an additional 5 minutes until the cheese has melted. Serve immediately.

Taco Casserole with Cheese

(Ready in about 25 minutes | Servings 4)

449 Calories; 23g Fat; 5.6g Carbs; 54g Protein; 3.2g Sugars

Ingredients

1 pound lean ground pork
1/2 pound ground beef
1/4 cup tomato puree
Sea salt and ground black pepper, to taste
1 teaspoon smoked paprika
1/2 teaspoon dried oregano
1 teaspoon dried basil
1 teaspoon dried rosemary
2 eggs
1 cup Cottage cheese, crumbled, at room temperature
1/2 cup Cotija cheese, shredded

Directions

Lightly grease a casserole dish with a nonstick cooking oil. Add the ground meat to the bottom of your casserole dish.
Add the tomato puree. Sprinkle with salt, black pepper, paprika, oregano, basil, and rosemary.
In a mixing bowl, whisk the egg with cheese. Place on top of the ground meat mixture. Place a piece of foil on top.
Bake in the preheated Air Fryer at 350 degrees F for 10 minutes; remove the foil and cook an additional 6 minutes. Bon appétit!

Beef

Cuban Mojo Beef

(Ready in about 15 minutes | Servings 3)

263 Calories; 17.4g Fat; 4.1g Carbs; 23.5g Protein; 2g Sugars

Ingredients

3/4 pound blade steak, cut into cubes
1 teaspoon olive oil
Salt and red pepper flakes, to season
Mojo sauce:
1 teaspoon garlic, smashed
2 tablespoons extra-virgin olive oil
2 tablespoons fresh parsley, chopped
2 tablespoons fresh cilantro, chopped
1/2 lime, freshly squeezed
1 green chili pepper, minced

Directions

Toss the steak with olive oil, salt and red pepper.
Cook in your Air Fryer at 400 degrees F for 12 minutes, turning
them over halfway through the cooking time.
Meanwhile, make the sauce by mixing all ingredients in your food
processor or blender. Serve the warm blade steak with the Mojo
sauce on the side. Enjoy!

Classic Beef Ribs

(Ready in about 35 minutes | Servings 4)

532 Calories; 39g Fat; 0.4g Carbs; 44.7g Protein; 0g Sugars

Ingredients

2 pounds beef back ribs
1 tablespoon sunflower oil
1/2 teaspoon mixed peppercorns, cracked
1 teaspoon red pepper flakes
1 teaspoon dry mustard
Coarse sea salt, to taste

Directions

Trim the excess fat from the beef ribs. Mix the sunflower oil,
cracked peppercorns, red pepper, dry mustard, and salt.
Rub over the ribs.
Cook in the preheated Air Fryer at 395 degrees F for 11 minutes
Turn the heat to 330 degrees F and continue to cook for 18 minutes
more. Serve warm.

Italian Sausage Peperonata Pomodoro

(Ready in about 15 minutes | Servings 2)

473 Calories; 34.6g Fat; 19.3g Carbs; 22.1g Protein; 9.7g Sugars

Ingredients

2 bell peppers, sliced
1 chili pepper
1 yellow onion, sliced
2 smoked beef sausages
1 teaspoon olive oil
2 medium-sized tomatoes, peeled and crushed
1 garlic clove, minced
1 teaspoon Italian spice mix

Directions

Spritz the sides and bottom of the cooking basket with a nonstick cooking oil. Add the peppers, onion and sausage to the cooking basket.

Cook at 390 degrees F for 10 minutes, shaking the basket periodically. Reserve.

Heat the olive oil in a medium-sized saucepan over medium-high flame until sizzling; add in the tomatoes and garlic; let it cook for 2 to 3 minutes.

Stir in the peppers, onion and Italian spice mix. Continue to cook for 1 minute longer or until heated through. Fold in the sausages and serve warm. Bon appétit!

Minty Tender Filet Mignon

(Ready in about 20 minutes + marinating time | Servings 4)

389 Calories; 20.4g Fat; 4.6g Carbs; 47.3g Protein; 1.7g Sugars

Ingredients

2 tablespoons olive oil
2 tablespoons Worcestershire sauce
1 lemon, juiced
1/4 cup fresh mint leaves, chopped
4 cloves garlic, minced
Sea salt and ground black pepper, to taste
2 pounds filet mignon

Directions

In a ceramic bowl, place the olive oil, Worcestershire sauce, lemon
juice, mint leaves, garlic, salt, black pepper, and cayenne pepper.
Add the fillet mignon and let it marinate for 2 hours in the
refrigerator.
Roast in the preheated Air Fryer at 400 degrees F for 18 minutes,
basting with the reserved marinade and flipping a couple of times.
Serve warm. Bon appétit!

Meatballs with Cranberry Sauce

(Ready in about 40 minutes | Servings 4)

520 Calories; 22.4g Fat; 44g Carbs; 45.4g Protein; 25.5g Sugars

Ingredients

Meatballs:
1 ½ pounds ground chuck
1 egg
1 cup rolled oats
1/2 cup Romano cheese, grated
1/2 teaspoon dried basil
1/2 teaspoon dried oregano
1 teaspoon paprika
2 garlic cloves, minced
2 tablespoons scallions, chopped
Sea salt and cracked black pepper, to taste
Cranberry Sauce:
10 ounces BBQ sauce
8 ounces cranberry sauce

Directions

In a large bowl, mix all ingredients for the meatballs. Mix until everything is well incorporated; then, shape the meat mixture into 2-inch balls using a cookie scoop. Transfer them to the lightly greased cooking basket and cook at 380 degrees F for 10 minutes. Shake the basket occasionally and work in batches. Add the BBQ sauce and cranberry sauce to a saucepan and cook over moderate heat until you achieve a glaze-like consistency; it will take about 15 minutes. Gently stir in the air fried meatballs and cook an additional 3 minutes or until heated through. Enjoy!

Fish

Salmon with Baby Bok Choy

(Ready in about 20 minutes | Servings 3)

308 Calories; 13.6g Fat; 12.2g Carbs; 34.3g Protein; 9.3g Sugars

Ingredients

1 pound salmon filets
1 teaspoon garlic chili paste
1 teaspoon sesame oil
1 tablespoon honey
1 tablespoon soy sauce
1 pound baby Bok choy, bottoms removed
Kosher salt and black pepper, to taste

Directions

Start by preheating your Air Fryer to 380 degrees F.
Toss the salmon fillets with garlic chili paste, sesame oil, honey, soy sauce, salt and black pepper.
Cook the salmon in the preheated Air Fryer for 6 minutes; turn the filets over and cook an additional 6 minutes.
Then, cook the baby Bok choy at 350 degrees F for 3 minutes; shake the basket and cook an additional 3 minutes. Salt and pepper to taste.
Serve the salmon fillets with the roasted baby Bok choy. Enjoy!

Mediterranean Calamari Salad

(Ready in about 15 minutes | Servings 3)

457 Calories; 31.3g Fat; 18.4g Carbs; 25.1g Protein; 9.2g Sugars

Ingredients

1 pound squid, cleaned, sliced into rings
2 tablespoons sherry wine
1/2 teaspoon granulated garlic
Salt, to taste
1/2 teaspoon ground black pepper
1/2 teaspoon basil
1/2 teaspoon dried rosemary
1 cup grape tomatoes
1 small red onion, thinly sliced
1/3 cup Kalamata olives, pitted and sliced
1/2 cup mayonnaise
1 teaspoon yellow mustard
1/2 cup fresh flat-leaf parsley leaves, coarsely chopped

Directions

Start by preheating the Air Fryer to 400 degrees F. Spritz the Air Fryer basket with cooking oil.

Toss the squid rings with the sherry wine, garlic, salt, pepper, basil, and rosemary. Cook in the preheated Air Fryer for 5 minutes, shaking the basket halfway through the cooking time.

Work in batches and let it cool to room temperature. When the squid is cool enough, add the remaining ingredients.

Gently stir to combine and serve well chilled. Bon appétit!

Shrimp Kabobs with Cherry Tomatoes

(Ready in about 30 minutes | Servings 4)

267 Calories; 6.8g Fat; 18.1g Carbs; 35.4g Protein; 14.5g Sugars

Ingredients

1 ½ pounds jumbo shrimp, cleaned, shelled and deveined
1 pound cherry tomatoes
2 tablespoons butter, melted
1 tablespoons Sriracha sauce
Sea salt and ground black pepper, to taste
1/2 teaspoon dried oregano
1/2 teaspoon dried basil
1 teaspoon dried parsley flakes
1/2 teaspoon marjoram
1/2 teaspoon mustard seeds

Directions

Toss all ingredients in a mixing bowl until the shrimp and tomatoes are covered on all sides.
Soak the wooden skewers in water for 15 minutes.
Thread the jumbo shrimp and cherry tomatoes onto skewers. Cook in the preheated Air Fryer at 400 degrees F for 5 minutes, working with batches. Bon appétit!

Anchovy and Cheese Wontons

(Ready in about 15 minutes | Servings 2)

473 Calories; 25.1g Fat; 19.4g Carbs; 41g Protein; 4.9g Sugars

Ingredients

1/2 pound anchovies
1/2 cup cheddar cheese, grated
1 cup fresh spinach
2 tablespoons scallions, minced
1 teaspoon garlic, minced
1 tablespoon Shoyu sauce
Himalayan salt and ground black pepper, to taste
1/2 pound wonton wrappers
1 teaspoon sesame oil

Directions

Mash the anchovies and mix with the cheese, spinach, scallions, garlic and Shoyu sauce; season with salt and black pepper and mix to combine well.

Fill your wontons with 1 tablespoon of the filling mixture and fold into triangle shape; brush the side with a bit of oil and water to seal the edges.

Cook in your Air Fryer at 390 degrees F for 10 minutes, flipping the wontons for even cooking. Enj

Sea Bass with French Sauce Tartare

(Ready in about 15 minutes | Servings 2)

384 Calories; 28.5g Fat; 3.5g Carbs; 27.6g Protein; 1g Sugars

Ingredients

1 tablespoon olive oil
2 sea bass fillets
Sauce:
1/2 cup mayonnaise
1 tablespoon capers, drained and chopped
1 tablespoon gherkins, drained and chopped
2 tablespoons scallions, finely chopped
2 tablespoons lemon juice

Directions

Start by preheating your Air Fryer to 395 degrees F. Drizzle olive oil all over the fish fillets.

Cook the sea bass in the preheated Air Fryer for 10 minutes, flipping them halfway through the cooking time.

Meanwhile, make the sauce by whisking the remaining ingredients until everything is well incorporated. Place in the refrigerator until ready to serve. Bon appétit!

Vegetable and Side Dishes

Classic Roasted Potatoes with Scallion Dip

(Ready in about 15 minutes | Servings 2)

567 Calories; 27g Fat; 72g Carbs; 11.3g Protein; 8.1g Sugars

Ingredients

4 medium-sized potatoes, peeled and cut into wedges
1 tablespoon olive oil
1/2 teaspoon ancho chili powder
1/2 teaspoon dried marjoram
1/2 teaspoon dried basil
Sea salt and ground black pepper, to taste
1/2 cup cream cheese
3 tablespoons scallions, sliced

Directions

Toss the potatoes with olive oil and spices until well coated.
Transfer them to the Air Fryer basket and cook at 400 degrees F for
6 minutes; shake the basket and cook for a further 6 minutes.
Meanwhile, whisk the cheese with the scallions and place the sauce
in your refrigerator until ready to use.
Serve the warm potatoes with the sauce for dipping. Bon appétit!

Greek-Style Roasted Tomatoes with Feta

(Ready in about 20 minutes | Servings 2)

148 Calories; 9.4g Fat; 9.4g Carbs; 7.8g Protein; 6.6g Sugars

Ingredients

3 medium-sized tomatoes, cut into four slices, pat dry
1 teaspoon dried basil
1 teaspoon dried oregano
1/4 teaspoon red pepper flakes, crushed
1/2 teaspoon sea salt
3 slices Feta cheese

Directions

Spritz the tomatoes with cooking oil and transfer them to the Air
Fryer basket. Sprinkle with seasonings.
Cook at 350 degrees F approximately 8 minutes turning them over
halfway through the cooking time.
Top with the cheese and cook an additional 4 minutes. Bon appétit!

Roasted Broccoli and Cauliflower with Tahini Sauce

(Ready in about 15 minutes | Servings 3)

178 Calories; 11.9g Fat; 14.6g Carbs; 6.8g Protein; 4.8g Sugars

Ingredients

1/2 pound broccoli, broken into florets
1/2 pound cauliflower, broken into florets
1 teaspoon onion powder
1/2 teaspoon porcini powder
1/4 teaspoon cumin powder
1/2 teaspoon granulated garlic
1 teaspoon olive oil
3 tablespoons tahini
2 tablespoons soy sauce
1 teaspoon white vinegar
Salt and chili flakes, to taste

Directions

Start by preheating your Air Fryer to 400 degrees F.
Now, toss the vegetables with the onion powder, porcini powder cumin powder, garlic and olive oil. Transfer your vegetables to the lightly greased cooking basket.
Air Fry your veggies in the preheated Air Fryer at 400 degrees F for 6 minutes. Remove the broccoli florets from the cooking basket.
Continue to cook the cauliflower for 5 to 6 minutes more.
Meanwhile, make the tahini sauce by simply whisking the remaining ingredients in a small bowl.
Spoon the sauce over the warm vegetables and serve immediately.
Bon appétit!

Spicy Ricotta Stuffed Mushrooms

(Ready in about 35 minutes | Servings 4)

214 Calories; 5.6g Fat; 30.4g Carbs; 12.3g Protein; 5g Sugars

Ingredients

1/2 pound small white mushrooms
Sea salt and ground black pepper, to taste
1 tablespoons Ricotta cheese
1/2 teaspoon ancho chili powder
1 teaspoon paprika
4 tablespoons all-purpose flour
1 egg
1/2 cup fresh breadcrumbs

Directions

Remove the stems from the mushroom caps and chop them; mix the chopped mushrooms steams with the salt, black pepper, cheese, chili powder, and paprika.
Stuff the mushroom caps with the cheese filling.
Place the flour in a shallow bowl, and beat the egg in another bowl. Place the breadcrumbs in a third shallow bowl.
Dip the mushrooms in the flour, then, dip in the egg mixture; finally, dredge in the breadcrumbs and press to adhere. Spritz the stuffed mushrooms with cooking spray.
Cook in the preheated Air Fryer at 360 degrees F for 18 minutes.
Bon appétit!

Italian Peperonata Classica

(Ready in about 25 minutes | Servings 4)

389 Calories; 18.4g Fat; 49.1g Carbs; 9.3g Protein; 19.8g Sugars

Ingredients

1 tablespoons olive oil
4 bell peppers, seeded and sliced
1 serrano pepper, seeded and sliced
1/2 cup onion, peeled and sliced
2 garlic cloves, crushed
2 tomatoes, pureed
2 tablespoons tomato ketchup
Sea salt and black pepper
1 teaspoon cayenne pepper
4 fresh basil leaves
10 Sicilian olives green, pitted and sliced
2 Ciabatta rolls

Directions

Brush the sides and bottom of the cooking basket with 1 tablespoon of olive oil. Add the peppers, onions, and garlic to the cooking basket. Cook for 5 minutes or until tender.

Add the tomatoes, ketchup, salt, black pepper, and cayenne pepper; add the remaining tablespoon of olive oil and cook in the preheated Air Fryer at 380 degrees F for 15 minutes, stirring occasionally.

Divide between individual bowls and garnish with basil leaves and olives. Serve with the Ciabatta rolls. Bon appétit!

SNACKS & APPETIZER

Paprika Potato Chips

(Ready in about 50 minutes | Servings 3)

190 Calories; 0.3g Fat; 43.8g Carbs; 4.7g Protein; 6.1g Sugars

Ingredients

3 potatoes, thinly sliced
1 teaspoon sea salt
1 teaspoon garlic powder
1 teaspoon paprika
1/4 cup ketchup

Directions

Add the sliced potatoes to a bowl with salted water. Let them soak
for 30 minutes. Drain and rinse your potatoes.
Pat dry and toss with salt.
Cook in the preheated Air Fryer at 400 degrees F for 15 minutes,
shaking the basket occasionally.
Work in batches. Toss with the garlic powder and paprika. Serve
with ketchup. Enjoy!

Cauliflower Bombs with Sweet & Sour Sauce

(Ready in about 25 minutes | Servings 4)

156 Calories; 11.9g Fat; 7.2g Carbs; 6.9g Protein; 3.3g Sugars

Ingredients

Cauliflower Bombs:
1/2 pound cauliflower
2 ounces Ricotta cheese
1/3 cup Swiss cheese
1 egg
1 tablespoon Italian seasoning mix
Sweet & Sour Sauce:
1 red bell pepper, jarred
1 clove garlic, minced
1 teaspoon sherry vinegar
1 tablespoon tomato puree
2 tablespoons olive oil
Salt and black pepper, to taste

Directions

Blanch the cauliflower in salted boiling water about 3 to 4 minutes until al dente. Drain well and pulse in a food processor.
Add the remaining ingredients for the cauliflower bombs; mix to combine well.
Bake in the preheated Air Fryer at 375 degrees F for 16 minutes, shaking halfway through the cooking time.
In the meantime, pulse all ingredients for the sauce in your food processor until combined. Season to taste. Serve the cauliflower bombs with the Sweet & Sour Sauce on the side. Bon appétit!

Pork Crackling with Sriracha Dip

(Ready in about 40 minutes | Servings 3)

525 Calories; 49.8g Fat; 10.6g Carbs; 6.8g Protein; 5.6g Sugars

Ingredients

1/2 pound pork rind
Sea salt and ground black pepper, to taste
1/2 cup tomato sauce
1 teaspoon Sriracha sauce
1/2 teaspoon stone-ground mustard

Directions

Rub sea salt and pepper on the skin side of the pork rind. Allow it to sit for 30 minutes.
Then, cut the pork rind into chunks using kitchen scissors.
Roast the pork rind at 380 degrees F for 8 minutes; turn them over and cook for a further 8 minutes or until blistered.
Meanwhile, mix the tomato sauce with the Sriracha sauce and mustard. Serve the pork crackling with the Sriracha dip and enjoy!

Easy and Delicious Pizza Puffs

(Ready in about 15 minutes | Servings 6)

186 Calories; 12g Fat; 12.4g Carbs; 6.5g Protein; 3.6g Sugars

Ingredients

6 ounces crescent roll dough

1/2 cup mozzarella cheese, shredded

3 ounces pepperoni

3 ounces mushrooms, chopped

1 teaspoon oregano

1 teaspoon garlic powder

1/4 cup Marina sauce, for dipping

Directions

Unroll the crescent dough. Roll out the dough using a rolling pin; cut into 6 pieces.

Place the cheese, pepperoni, and mushrooms in the center of each pizza puff. Sprinkle with oregano and garlic powder.

Fold each corner over the filling using wet hands. Press together to cover the filling entirely and seal the edges.

Now, spritz the bottom of the Air Fryer basket with cooking oil. Lay the pizza puffs in a single layer in the cooking basket. Work in batches.

Bake at 370 degrees F for 5 to 6 minutes or until golden brown.

Serve with the marinara sauce for dipping.

Mexican Cheesy Zucchini Bites

(Ready in about 25 minutes | Servings 4)

231 Calories; 9g Fat; 29.3g Carbs; 8.4g Protein; 2.3g Sugars

Ingredients

1 large-sized zucchini, thinly sliced
1/2 cup flour
1/4 cup yellow cornmeal
1 egg, whisked
1/2 cup tortilla chips, crushed
1/2 cup Queso Añejo, grated
Salt and cracked pepper, to taste

Directions

Pat dry the zucchini slices with a kitchen towel.
Mix the remaining ingredients in a shallow bowl; mix until everything is well combined. Dip each zucchini slice in the prepared batter.
Cook in the preheated Air Fryer at 400 degrees F for 12 minutes, shaking the basket halfway through the cooking time.
Work in batches until the zucchini slices are crispy and golden brown. Enjoy!

Rice and Grains

Mexican-Style Bubble Loaf

(Ready in about 20 minutes | Servings 4)

382 Calories; 17.5g Fat; 50.8g Carbs; 7.1g Protein; 6g Sugars

Ingredients

1 (16-ounce) can flaky buttermilk biscuits
4 tablespoons olive oil, melted
1/2 cup Manchego cheese, grated
1/2 teaspoon granulated garlic
1 tablespoon fresh cilantro, chopped
1/2 teaspoon Mexican oregano
1 teaspoon chili pepper flakes
Kosher salt and ground black pepper, to taste

Directions

Open a can of biscuits and cut each biscuit into quarters. Brush each piece of biscuit with the olive oil and begin layering in a lightly greased Bundt pan.
Cover the bottom of the pan with one layer of biscuits.
Next, top the first layer with half of the cheese, spices and granulated garlic. Repeat for another layer.
Finish with a third layer of dough.
Cook your bubble loaf in the Air Fryer at 330 degrees for about 15 minutes until the cheese is bubbly. Bon appétit!

Delicious Sultana Muffins

(Ready in about 20 minutes | Servings 4)

288 Calories; 9.5g Fat; 44.3g Carbs; 6.7g Protein; 18.5g Sugars

Ingredients

1 cup flour
1 teaspoon baking powder
1tablespoon honey
1 egg
1/2 teaspoon star anise, ground
1 teaspoon vanilla extract
1 egg
1/2 cup milk
2 tablespoons melted butter
1 cup dried Sultanas, soaked in
2 tablespoons of rum

Directions

Mix all the ingredients until everything is well incorporated. Spritz a silicone muffin tin with cooking spray.
Pour the batter into the silicone muffin tin.
Bake in the preheated Air Fryer at 330 degrees F for 12 to 15 minutes. Rotate the silicone muffin tin halfway through the cooking time to ensure even cooking.
Bon appétit!

Healthy Oatmeal Cups

(Ready in about 15 minutes | Servings 2)

294 Calories; 8.5g Fat; 47.2g Carbs; 10.2g Protein; 25.4g Sugars

Ingredients

1 large banana, mashed
1 cup quick-cooking steel cut oats
1 tablespoon agave syrup
1 egg, well beaten
1 cup coconut milk
3 ounces mixed berries

Directions

In a mixing bowl, thoroughly combine the banana, oats, agave syrup, beaten egg and coconut milk.
Spoon the mixture into an Air Fryer safe baking dish.
Bake in the preheated Air Fryer at 395 degrees F for about 7 minutes. Top with berries and continue to bake an additional 2 minutes.
Spoon into individual bowls and serve with a splash of coconut milk if desired. Bon appétit!

Baked Tortilla Chips

(Ready in about 15 minutes | Servings 3)

167 Calories; 6.1g Fat; 26.4g Carbs; 3.2g Protein; 0.5g Sugars

Ingredients

1/2 (12-ounce) package corn tortillas
1 tablespoon canola oil
1/2 teaspoon chili powder
1 teaspoon salt

Directions

Cut the tortillas into small rounds using a cookie cutter.
Brush the rounds with canola oil. Sprinkle them with chili powder and salt.
Transfer to the lightly greased Air Fryer basket and bake at 360 degrees F for 5 minutes, shaking the basket halfway through. Bake until the chips are crisp, working in batches.
Serve with salsa or guacamole. Enjoy!

Mexican-Style Brown Rice Casserole

(Ready in about 50 minutes | Servings 4)

433 Calories; 7.4g Fat; 79.6g Carbs; 12.1g Protein; 2.8g Sugars

Ingredients

1 tablespoon olive oil
1 shallot, chopped
2 cloves garlic, minced
1 habanero pepper, minced
2 cups brown rice
3 cups chicken broth
1 cup water
2 ripe tomatoes, pureed
Sea salt and ground black pepper, to taste
1/2 teaspoon dried Mexican oregano
1 teaspoon red pepper flakes
1 cup Mexican Cotija cheese, crumbled

Directions

In a nonstick skillet, heat the olive oil over a moderate flame. Once hot, cook the shallot, garlic, and habanero pepper until tender and fragrant; reserve. Heat the brown rice, vegetable broth and water in a pot over high heat. Bring it to a boil; turn the stove down to simmer and cook for 35 minutes. Grease a baking pan with nonstick cooking spray. Spoon the cooked rice into the baking pan. Add the sautéed mixture. Spoon the tomato puree over the sautéed mixture. Sprinkle with salt, black pepper, oregano, and red pepper.
Cook in the preheated Air Fryer at 380 degrees F for 8 minutes. Top with the Cotija cheese and bake for 5 minutes longer or until cheese is melted. Enjoy

---

Vegan

The Best Crispy Tofu

(Ready in about 55 minutes | Servings 4)

245 Calories; 13.3g Fat; 16.7g Carbs; 18.2g Protein; 1.2g Sugars

Ingredients

16 ounces firm tofu, pressed and cubed
1 tablespoon vegan oyster sauce
1 tablespoon tamari sauce
1 teaspoon cider vinegar
1 teaspoon pure maple syrup
1 teaspoon sriracha
1/2 teaspoon shallot powder
1/2 teaspoon porcini powder
1 teaspoon garlic powder
1 tablespoon sesame oil
5 tablespoons cornstarch

Directions

Toss the tofu with the oyster sauce, tamari sauce, vinegar, maple syrup, sriracha, shallot powder, porcini powder, garlic powder, and sesame oil. Let it marinate for 30 minutes.
Toss the marinated tofu with the cornstarch.
Cook at 360 degrees F for 10 minutes; turn them over and cook for 12 minutes more. Bon appétit!

Mashed Potatoes with Roasted Peppers

(Ready in about 1 hour | Servings 4)

490 Calories; 17g Fat; 79.1g Carbs; 10.5g Protein; 9.8g Sugars

Ingredients

4 potatoes
1 tablespoon vegan margarine
1 teaspoon garlic powder
1 pound bell peppers, seeded and quartered lengthwise
2 Fresno peppers, seeded and halved lengthwise
4 tablespoons olive oil
2 tablespoons cider vinegar
4 garlic cloves, pressed
Kosher salt, to taste
1/2 teaspoon freshly ground black pepper
1/2 teaspoon dried dill

Directions

Place the potatoes in the Air Fryer basket and cook at 400 degrees F for 40 minutes. Discard the skin and mash the potatoes with the vegan margarine and garlic powder.

Then, roast the peppers at 400 degrees F for 5 minutes. Give the peppers a half turn; place them back in the cooking basket and roast for another 5 minutes.

Turn them one more time and roast until the skin is charred and soft or 5 more minutes. Peel the peppers and let them cool to room temperature.

Toss your peppers with the remaining ingredients and serve with the mashed potatoes. Bon appétit!

Paprika Squash Fries

(Ready in about 15 minutes | Servings 3)

202 Calories; 5.8g Fat; 30.2g Carbs; 8.1g Protein; 2.9g Sugars

Ingredients

1/4 cup rice milk
1/4 cup almond flour
1 tablespoons nutritional yeast
1/4 teaspoon shallot powder
1/2 teaspoon garlic powder
1/2 teaspoon paprika
Sea salt and ground black pepper, to taste
1 pound butternut squash, peeled and into sticks
1 cup tortilla chips, crushed

Directions

In a bowl, thoroughly combine the milk flour, nutritional yeast and spices. In another shallow bowl, place the crushed tortilla chips.
Dip the butternut squash sticks into the batter and then, roll them over the crushed tortilla chips until well coated.
Arrange the squash pieces in the Air Fryer cooking basket. Cook the squash fries at 400 degrees F for about 12 minutes, shaking the basket once or twice. Bon appétit!

Baked Spicy Tortilla Chips

(Ready in about 20 minutes | Servings 3)

189 Calories; 5.1g Fat; 30.7g Carbs; 4.7g Protein; 2g Sugars

Ingredients

6 (6-inch) corn tortillas
1 teaspoon canola oil
1 teaspoon salt
1/4 teaspoon ground white pepper
1/2 teaspoon ground cumin
1/2 teaspoon ancho chili powder

Directions

Slice the tortillas into quarters. Brush the tortilla pieces with the canola oil until well coated.
Toss with the spices and transfer to the Air Fryer basket.
Bake at 360 degrees F for 8 minutes or until lightly golden. Work in batches. Bon appétit!

Authentic Churros with Hot Chocolate

(Ready in about 25 minutes | Servings 3)

432 Calories; 15.8g Fat; 63.9g Carbs; 8.4g Protein; 24.7g Sugars

Ingredients

1/2 cup water

2 tablespoons granulated sugar

1/4 teaspoon sea salt

1 teaspoon lemon zest

1 tablespoon canola oil

1 cup all-purpose flour

2 ounces dark chocolate

1 cup milk

1 tablespoon cornstarch

1/3 cup sugar

1 teaspoon ground cinnamon

Directions

To make the churro dough, boil the water in a pan over medium-high heat; now, add the sugar, salt and lemon zest; cook until dissolved.

Add the canola oil and remove the pan from the heat. Gradually stir in the flour, whisking continuously until the mixture forms a ball.

Pour the mixture into a piping bag with a large star tip. Squeeze 4-inch strips of dough into the greased Air Fryer pan.

Cook at 410 degrees F for 6 minutes.

Meanwhile, prepare the hot chocolate for dipping. Melt the chocolate and 1/2 cup of milk in a pan over low heat.

Dissolve the cornstarch in the remaining 1/2 cup of milk; stir into the hot chocolate mixture.

Cook on low heat approximately 5 minutes.

Mix the sugar and cinnamon; roll the churros in this mixture. Serve with the hot chocolate on the side. Enjoy!

Dessert

Perfect English-Style Scones

(Ready in about 15 minutes | Servings 4)

458 Calories; 25g Fat; 47.1g Carbs; 6.8g Protein; 7.9g Sugars

Ingredients

1 ½ cups cake flour
1/4 cup caster sugar
1 teaspoon baking powder
1 teaspoon baking soda
1/4 teaspoon salt
1/2 teaspoon vanilla essence
1/2 stick butter
1 egg, beaten
1/2 cup almond milk

Directions

Start by preheating your Air Fryer to 360 degrees F.
Thoroughly combine all dry ingredients. In another bowl, combine all wet ingredients. Then, add the wet mixture to the dry ingredients and stir to combine well.
Roll your dough out into a circle and cut into wedges.
Bake the scones in the preheated Air Fryer for about 11 minutes, flipping them halfway through the cooking time. Bon appétit!

Fried Honey Banana

(Ready in about 20 minutes | Servings 2)

363 Calories; 14.3g Fat; 61.1g Carbs; 3.7g Protein; 33.3g Sugars

Ingredients

1 ripe bananas, peeled and sliced
2 tablespoons honey
3 tablespoons rice flour
3 tablespoons desiccated coconut
A pinch of fine sea salt
1/2 teaspoon baking powder
1/4 teaspoon cardamom powder

Directions

Preheat the Air Fryer to 390 degrees F.
Drizzle honey over the banana slices.
In a mixing dish, thoroughly combine the rice flour, coconut, salt, baking powder, and cardamom powder. Roll each slice of banana over the flour mixture.
Bake in the preheated Air Fryer approximately 13 minutes, flipping them halfway through the cooking time. Bon appétit!

Mini Apple and Cranberry Crisp Cakes

(Ready in about 40 minutes | Servings 3)

338 Calories; 17.5g Fat; 41.9g Carbs; 5.2g Protein; 18.1g Sugars

Ingredients

2 Bramley cooking apples, peeled, cored and chopped
1/4 cup dried cranberries
1 teaspoon fresh lemon juice
1 tablespoon golden caster sugar
1 teaspoon apple pie spice mix
A pinch of coarse salt
1/2 cup rolled oats
1/3 cup brown bread crumbs
1/4 cup butter, diced

Directions

Divide the apples and cranberries between three lightly greased
ramekins. Drizzle your fruits with lemon juice and sprinkle with
caster sugar, spice mix and salt.
Then, make the streusel by mixing the remaining ingredients in a
bowl. Spread the streusel batter on top of the filling.
Bake the mini crisp cakes in the preheated Air Fryer at 330 degrees F
for 35 minutes or until they're a dark golden brown around the
edges.
Bon appétit!

Grilled Banana Boats

(Ready in about 15 minutes | Servings 3)

269 Calories; 5.9g Fat; 47.9g Carbs; 2.6g Protein; 28.3g Sugars

Ingredients

2 large bananas

1 tablespoon ginger snaps

2 tablespoons mini chocolate chips

3 tablespoons mini marshmallows

3 tablespoons crushed vanilla wafers

Directions

In the peel, slice your banana lengthwise; make sure not to slice all the way through the banana. Divide the remaining ingredients between the banana pockets.

Place in the Air Fryer grill pan. Cook at 395 degrees F for 7 minutes. Let the banana boats cool for 5 to 6 minutes, and then eat with a spoon. Bon appétit!

Coconut Cheesecake Bites

(Ready in about 25 minutes + chilling time | Servings 8)

415 Calories; 32.3g Fat; 26.4g Carbs; 6.8g Protein; 17.1g Sugars

Ingredients

1 ½ cups Oreo cookies, crushed

4 ounces granulated sugar

4 tablespoons butter, softened

12 ounces cream cheese

4 ounces double cream

2 eggs, lightly whisked

1 teaspoon pure vanilla extract

1 teaspoon pure coconut extract

1 cup toasted coconut

Directions

Start by preheating your Air Fryer to 350 degrees F.

Mix the crushed Oreos with sugar and butter; press the crust into silicone cupcake molds. Bake for 5 minutes and allow them to cool on wire racks.

Using an electric mixer, whip the cream cheese and double cream until fluffy; add one egg at a time and continue to beat until creamy. Finally, add the vanilla and coconut extract.

Pour the topping mixture on top of the crust. Bake at 320 degrees F for 13 to 15 minutes.

Afterwards, top with the toasted coconut. Allow the mini cheesecakes to chill in your refrigerator before serving. Bon appétit!

Other Air Fryer Recipes

Greek Meatballs

(Ready in about 15 minutes | Servings 2)

493 Calories; 27.9g Fat; 27.1g Carbs; 32.6g Protein; 4.2g Sugars

Ingredients

1/2 pound ground chicken
1 egg
1 slice stale bread, cubed and soaked in milk
1 teaspoon fresh garlic, pressed
2 tablespoons Romano cheese, grated
1 bell pepper, deveined and chopped
1 teaspoon olive oil
1/2 teaspoon dried oregano
1/2 teaspoon dried basil
1/8 teaspoon grated nutmeg
Sea salt and ground black pepper, to taste
2 pita bread

Directions

Thoroughly combine all ingredients, except for the pita bread, in a mixing bowl. Stir until everything is well incorporated.
Roll the mixture into 6 meatballs and place them in a lightly oiled cooking basket.
Air fry at 380 degrees F for 10 minutes, shaking the basket occasionally to ensure even cooking.
Place the keftedes in a pita bread and serve with tomato and tzatziki sauce if desired.

Pork with Roasted Peppers

(Ready in about 55 minutes | Servings 3)

409 Calories; 20.1g Fat; 4.3g Carbs; 49g Protein; 2.4g Sugars

Ingredients

1 red bell peppers
1 ½ pounds pork loin
1 garlic clove, halved
1 teaspoon lard, melted
1/2 teaspoon cayenne pepper
1/4 teaspoon cumin powder
1/4 teaspoon ground bay laurel
Kosher salt and ground black pepper, to taste

Directions

Roast the peppers in the preheated Air Fryer at 395 degrees F for 10 minutes, flipping them halfway through the cooking time.
Let them steam for 10 minutes; then, peel the skin and discard the stems and seeds. Slice the peppers into halves and add salt to taste.
Rub the pork with garlic; brush with melted lard and season with spices until well coated on all sides.
Place in the cooking basket and cook at 360 digress F for 25 minutes. Turn the meat over and cook an additional 20 minutes.
Serve with roasted peppers.

American Roast Beef

(Ready in about 30 minutes | Servings 3)

294 Calories; 10.9g Fat; 0.3g Carbs; 45.9g Protein; 0.3g Sugars

Ingredients

1 pound beef eye of round roast
1 teaspoon sesame oil
1 teaspoon red pepper flakes
1/4 teaspoon dried bay laurel
1/2 teaspoon cumin powder
Sea salt and black pepper, to taste
1 sprig thyme, crushed

Directions

Simply toss the beef with the remaining ingredients; toss until well coated on all sides.
Cook in the preheated Air Fryer at 390 degrees F for 15 to 20 minutes, flipping the meat halfway through to cook on the other side.
Remove from the cooking basket, cover loosely with foil and let rest for 15 minutes before carving and serving.

Meatballs with Fish and Peppers

(Ready in about 15 minutes | Servings 3)

226 Calories; 6.5g Fat; 10.9g Carbs; 31.4g Protein; 2.6g Sugars

Ingredients

1 pound haddock
1 egg
2 tablespoons milk
1 bell pepper, deveined and finely chopped
2 stalks fresh scallions, minced
1/2 teaspoon fresh garlic, minced
Sea salt and ground black pepper, to taste
1/2 teaspoon cumin seeds
1/4 teaspoon celery seeds
1/2 cup breadcrumbs
1 teaspoon olive oil

Directions

Thoroughly combine all ingredients, except for the breadcrumbs and olive oil, until everything is blended well.
Then, roll the mixture into 3 patties and coat them with breadcrumbs, pressing to adhere. Drizzle olive oil over the patties and transfer them to the Air Fryer cooking basket.
Cook the fish cakes at 400 degrees F for 5 minutes; turn them over and continue to cook an additional 5 minutes until cooked through.

Zucchini Pancakes

(Ready in about 20 minutes | Servings 3)

227 Calories; 11.5g Fat; 19.2g Carbs; 10.3g Protein; 1.9g Sugars

Ingredients

2 medium zucchini, shredded and drained
1 teaspoon Italian seasoning mix
Sea salt and ground black pepper, to taste
1/2 yellow onion, finely chopped
1 teaspoon garlic, finely chopped
1/2 cup plain flour
1 large egg, beaten
1/2 cup Asiago cheese, shredded
1 teaspoon olive oil

Directions

In a mixing bowl, thoroughly combine the zucchini, spices, yellow onion, garlic, flour, egg and Asiago cheese.
Shape the mixture into patties and brush them with olive oil; transfer the patties to a lightly oiled cooking basket.
Cook the patties in the preheated Air Fryer at 380 degrees F for 15 minutes, turning them over once or twice to ensure even cooking.
Garnish with some extra cheese if desired and serve at room temperature.

Pear Chips

(Ready in about 10 minutes | Servings 2)

94 Calories; 2.6g Fat; 18.1g Carbs; 0.7g Protein; 12.6g Sugars

Ingredients

1 large pear, cored and sliced
1 teaspoon apple pie spice blend
1 teaspoon coconut oil
1 teaspoon honey

Directions

Toss the pear slices with the spice blend, coconut oil and honey.
Then, place the pear slices in the Air Fryer cooking basket and cook
at 360 degrees F for about 8 minutes.
Shake the basket once or twice to ensure even cooking. Pear chips
will crisp up as it cools.

Monkey Bread

(Ready in about 15 minutes | Servings 3)

270 Calories; 9.5g Fat; 33.6g Carbs; 11.2g Protein; 6.1g Sugars

Ingredients

6 ounces refrigerated crescent rolls
¼ cup ketchup
¼ cup pesto sauce
½ cup provolone cheese, shredded
2 cloves garlic, minced
½ teaspoon dried oregano
½ teaspoon dried basil
½ teaspoon dried parsley flakes

Directions

Start by preheating your Air Fryer to 350 degrees F.
Roll out crescent rolls. Divide the ingredients between crescent rolls and roll them up. Using your fingertips, gently press them to seal the edges.
Bake the mini monkey bread for 12 minutes or until the top is golden brown.

Beet with Tahini Sauce

(Ready in about 40 minutes | Servings 2)

253 Calories; 18.1g Fat; 19.1g Carbs; 6.4g Protein; 10.1g Sugars

Ingredients

1 golden beets
1 tablespoon sesame oil
Sea salt and ground black pepper, to taste
2 cups baby spinach
2 tablespoons tahini
2 tablespoons soy sauce
1 tablespoon white vinegar
1 clove garlic, pressed
1/2 jalapeno pepper, chopped
1/4 teaspoon ground cumin

Directions

Toss the golden beets with sesame oil. Cook the golden beets in the preheated Air Fryer at 400 degrees F for 40 minutes, turning them over once or twice to ensure even cooking.

Let your beets cool completely and then, slice them with a sharp knife. Place the beets in a salad bowl and add in salt, pepper and baby spinach.

In a small mixing dish, whisk the remaining ingredients until well combined.

Spoon the sauce over your beets, toss to combine and serve immediately.

253 Calories; 18.1g Fat; 19.1g Carbs; 6.4g Protein; 10.1g Sugars

Fried Cupcakes

(Ready in about 10 minutes | Servings 4)

255 Calories; 7.6g Fat; 42.1g Carbs; 5g Protein; 17.1g Sugars

Ingredients

8 ounces bread dough
2 tablespoons butter, melted
2 ounces powdered sugar

Directions

Cut the dough into strips and twist them together 3 to 4 times. Then, brush the dough twists with melted butter and sprinkle sugar over them.
Cook the dough twists at 350 degrees F for 8 minutes, tossing the basket halfway through the cooking time.
Serve with your favorite dip.

CPSIA information can be obtained
at www.ICGtesting.com
Printed in the USA
LVHW050149260621
691221LV00001B/41